WHY OUR CHURCH SWITCHED TO THE ESV

Why Our Church Switched to the ESV

KEVIN DEYOUNG

CROSSWAY

WHEATON, ILLINOIS

Crossway is a publishing ministry of Good News Publishers.

BP			20	19	18	17	16	15	14	13
14	13	12	11	10	9	8	7	6	5	4	3	2

INTRODUCTION

I have been the Senior Pastor at University Reformed Church (URC) in East Lansing, Michigan, since the summer of 2004. Almost as soon as arrived I began hearing, "We need to replace the Bibles we use for worship. They are falling apart!" At the same time, and mostly unrelated, members of the congregation were asking me as their new pastor, "What Bible translation do you recommend?" Since we had the New International Version (NIV) in the pews at the time (actually for us, on the chairs), I usually said something like, "You know, there are a number of good translations. God can use almost all of them. Personally, I like the English Standard Version the best. I think it does the best job of being readable and as literal as possible."

Naturally, a second question would sometimes follow: "So why do we use the NIV in our services?" Not wanting to upset too many apple carts, I would explain that at some point in the future we would need to order new Bibles for worship, and at that time the elders would take a look at what translation could serve us best.

It took a few years, but eventually we had no choice but to replace our well-worn pew Bibles. And when the time came I did my best to gently persuade the elders, and the congregation after them, that the ESV was the best choice. This booklet explains why I wanted our church to switch to the ESV and why, with virtually no controversy, we eventually did.

Thousands of pages have been written about Bible translation theory and the merits and demerits of particular English translations of the Bible. Obviously, in this short space I can't begin to do justice to all the arguments and examples scholars have offered for one approach or another. My goal is much more modest. I want to give several reasons why I use the English Standard Version (ESV) in my own personal study and devotions and why we now use it in our worship services and educational ministries too.

But let me start with a few comments by way of introduction. First, it must be stated unequivocally that the Lord in his sovereignty has used and will continue to use many different English translations to build up his church. This isn't to say that all translations are the same or that it doesn't matter which translation we use. It's simply an acknowledgment that God's Word is sufficiently communicated in many different translations in such a way that people can come to saving faith in Jesus Christ. So in arguing for the ESV, please do not hear me belittling the work the Lord has accomplished through many other English translations.

Second, an attitude of thanksgiving should permeate this whole discussion. There are millions of people in the world who still do not have the Scriptures in a language they can understand and millions more who do not have the Bible in their heart language. How fortunate are English speakers who not only have 500 years of Bible translation history to rely on, but can choose from more than a dozen modern translations. Ours is an embarrassment of riches.

Third, my support for the ESV is not because I loathe other translations and certainly not because I haven't read from or been blessed by any other English translation. I've read portions of the Bible in the New Revised Standard Version (NRSV), New King James Version (NKJV), and The Message, and the entire Bible in a number of other translations. I grew up using the New International Version (NIV). This is what my church used, my parents read around the dinner table, and what I received when I graduated from children's church—a beloved illustrated gift Bible that I carried around until the binding fell apart. I've read through the NIV probably half a dozen times—all with great profit. In college, I started trying other translations. I read through the King James Version (KJV) three or four times and loved its stately beauty. I tried the Revised Standard Version (RSV) once and then moved on to the New American Standard Bible (NASB) because it was a very literal translation. After using the NASB for several years and reading through it several times, I switched to the ESV because it had precisely the balance I was looking for: more literal than the NIV and more readable than the NASB.

By now, I've read through the ESV a dozen times or so. Since switching for my own personal use, shortly after the ESV was released in 2001, I've never had any thoughts of going back to another translation. The same goes for preaching. I am thankful for all the sermons I had the privilege to preach using the NIV, but switching to the ESV—which I did several years ago when my congregation made the change—has made my job as a preacher easier and more enjoyable. I think our church has welcomed the change too.

My decision to switch to the ESV several years ago was not because I felt that all other translations were terrible but because I resonated with its translation philosophy. Since then, I have come to love the readability, accuracy, and style of the ESV. It's certainly not perfect; no translation is. But I hope it becomes the new "standard" among English speakers and becomes the Bible used for prayer, preaching, memorization, study, and worship in more and more churches.

Narrowing the Question

It would be impossible, in a few pages or even a few hundred pages, to compare the ESV with every other modern English translation. Instead, I want to focus on how the ESV compares with the NIV, the former pew Bible at University Reformed Church and the most popular Bible in the United States in terms of sales. I could give reasons why I like the ESV more than other translations—the KJV/NKJV is based on inferior manuscripts, the NASB is too wooden and lacking in literary quality, the NRSV opts for a gender-neutral approach, The Message is too paraphrastic, the RSV is burdened by theological bias, etc.—but since the switch at my church was from NIV to ESV, I will explain my preference for the ESV by way of comparison with the NIV.[1]

ESV OR NIV FOR URC?

Here are seven reasons why I prefer the ESV over the NIV.

1. The ESV employs an "essentially literal" translation philosophy. The NIV, by contrast, has a less literal "dynamic equivalence" philosophy (though it is probably the most literal of the dynamic equivalent translations). The difference means the ESV tries to translate "word-for-word" as much as possible while the NIV translates "thought-for-thought." The different approaches can be seen by comparing prefaces (italics added).

NIV Preface

The first concern of the translators has been the accuracy of the translation and its fidelity to the *thought* of the biblical writers. They have weighed the significance of the lexical and grammatical details of the Hebrew, Aramaic and Greek texts. At the same time, they have striven for *more than a word-for-word translation*. Because thought patterns and syntax

---

[1] In the spring of 2011, subsequent to our church's decision to change from the NIV to the ESV, the publishers of the NIV published a new edition of their translation. My comparisons of the ESV and NIV in this publication are based on the 1984 version of the NIV, on which our church's decision was based. In places where the wording of the 2011 revision of the NIV has some bearing on my comparison of the versions, that will be noted.

differ from language to language, faithful communication of the meaning of the writers of the Bible demands frequent modifications in sentence structure and constant regard for the contextual meaning of words (emphasis added).

ESV Preface

The ESV is an "essentially literal" translation that seeks as far as possible to capture the *precise wording* of the original text and the personal style of each biblical writer. As such, its *emphasis is on "word-for-word" correspondence*, at the same time taking into account differences of grammar, syntax, and idiom between current literary English and the original languages. Thus it seeks to be transparent to the original text, letting the reader see as directly as possible the structure and meaning of the original (emphasis added).

The difference between the NIV and ESV is not a chasm, but one of degree. Anyone who has translated from one language to another knows that achieving a rigid word-for-word translation is a naive goal. Languages work differently and the words fit together in different orders, making strict word-for-word translations overly clumsy and often impossible. That's why the ESV is called an *essentially* literal translation. Its goal is to translate word for word wherever possible. Because every single word of Scripture is breathed out by God and is for our edification (2 Tim. 3:16; 2 Pet. 1:20–21; see also Prov. 30:5; Matt. 4:4; 5:18; John 10:34), it is important to translate, insofar as possible, not just the thought of the biblical writers but the meaning that each word contributes to the sentence. If this talk about translation philosophy seems esoteric and abstract, the differences between the two approaches—essentially literal and dynamic equivalence—will be evident when we look at specific examples below.

2. The ESV is a more transparent translation. That is to say, the ESV leaves interpretive ambiguities unresolved so that the reader or preacher or student, rather than the translator, can determine which meaning is best. Often, even when the Greek or Hebrew construction can be easily translated, the meaning of the translation is still ambiguous. A common example in Greek involves genitives. The most basic translation for a noun in the genitive case would include the word "of." For example, 2 Corinthians 5:14 reads (in the ESV) "For the love of Christ controls us . . . " The phrase "the love of Christ" translates the Greek *agapē tou Christou* which is, grammatically, a nominative noun followed by a genitive noun. The love of Christ could mean the love Christ has for us, or the love we have for Christ, or both. All three are possible from the Greek and from the ESV translation. The NIV, however, translates 2 Corinthians 5:14 "For Christ's love compels us . . . " This may be what the Greek phrase means (or it may not be), but the NIV has settled the matter for us—*agapē tou Christou* means the love Christ has for us (i.e., "Christ's love")—and has not allowed the reader to come to his own conclusion. This is what I mean when I say the ESV is more transparent. It makes more of an effort to leave ambiguities in the English that are actually there in the Greek.

Here are several more examples:

James 2:12

[ESV] "So speak and so act as those who are to be judged under the law of liberty [*nomou eleutherias*]."

[NIV] "Speak and act as those who are going to be judged by the law that gives freedom."

The NIV interprets the law of liberty to mean the law that gives freedom, but the Greek is ambiguous. The phrase *nomou eleutherias* may mean that liberty is the law under which we are to be judged, or that liberty is characteristic of the law, or that the law imparts liberty, or some combination of all of the above. The ESV allows for all these possibilities; the NIV does not.

1 Thessalonians 1:3

[ESV] "remembering before our God and Father your work of faith [*tou ergou tēs pisteōs*] and labor of love [*tou kopou tēs agapēs*] and steadfastness of hope [*tēs hupomonēs tēs elpidos*] in our Lord Jesus Christ."

[NIV] "We continually remember before our God and Father your work produced by faith, your labor prompted by love, and your endurance inspired by hope in our Lord Jesus Christ."

Even without a knowledge of Greek, most readers will be able to see from this side-by-side comparison that the NIV has significantly augmented the passage. Of course, translations require plenty of judgment calls (it's not an exact science). Every translation effort involves some interpretation. But the NIV has tried too hard to clarify verses like this one by adding key words that are not in the Greek, such as "produced," "prompted," and "inspired."

Hebrews 6:1

[ESV] ". . . not laying again a foundation of repentance from dead works [*nekron ergon*] . . . "

[NIV] ". . . not laying again the foundation of repentance from acts that lead to death . . . "

Again, the NIV has removed the ambiguity that exists in the Greek and is made transparent in the ESV. Are dead works those works that lead to death, or those that are done in the absence of life, or both? The NIV decides the matter for us.

We see a similar example with "the love of God" (*agapē tou theou*) in 1 John, which can mean the love God has for us, or our love for God, or both. The ESV consistently translates the phrase "the love of God" while the NIV interprets the phrase as "God's love" (1 John 2:5), "God showed his love" (4:9), and "love for God" (5:3). The NIV approach gives the English reader not only a destabilized text (the same phrase translated three different ways) but interpretations in addition to translation.[2] Granted, the words or phrases do not always have to be translated the same way, but if "love of God" is understandable in each instance, why muddy the waters with interpretative amplifications?

Likewise, Romans 1:5 speaks of "the obedience of faith" (ESV). The Greek (*hupakoēn pisteōs*) may mean that obedience comes from faith, or that faith is obedience, or some combination of both. The NIV removes the ambiguity and renders the phrase "the obedience that comes from faith."

This whole notion of a "transparent" translation is a key difference in translation philosophy, and it affects a myriad of translation decisions.[3] Will ambiguities be left in the text or resolved? Will strange images and figures be decoded for the reader, or will we meet the text on its own terms, with its own way of speaking? Will important repetitions be removed or retained? Will implicit information be made explicit or left implicit for the reader to discover? Will immediate intelligibility trump almost all other considerations, or will we allow the "otherness" of an ancient, foreign book to shine through as much as possible? Should Bible translation be a guide through the forest of interpretive difficulties or a window that makes the original

---

[2] The 2011 revision of the NIV changed "God's love" (1 John 2:5) to "love for God."

[3] See C. John Collins, "What the Reader Wants and the Translator Can Give: First John as a Test Case," in Wayne Grudem, et al., *Translating Truth: The Case for Essentially Literal Bible Translation* (Wheaton, IL: Crossway, 2005). Included in this helpful book are chapters from Wayne Grudem, Leland Ryken, Vern Poythress, Bruce Winter, and a foreword by J. I. Packer. For more on "transparency" see Raymond C. Van Leeuwen, "We Really Do Need Another Bible Translation," *Christianity Today*, October 2001 (accessed August 31, 2010 at http://www.christianitytoday.com/ct/article_print.html?id=16366).

language, style, and ambiguity of the text as transparent as possible? I have to side with the ESV. When it comes to understanding and living by God's Word, I want teachers to teach and translations to be transparent.

3. The ESV engages in less over-translation. Translation is not always based on one-to-one correspondence. You cannot take a single word in one language and always use a single word in another language to translate it. Sometimes a word needs to be translated with two or three words. At other times two or three words in the original language require only one word for accurate translation. That's how translation works. But the NIV often adds words unnecessarily, not in order to better translate a Greek or Hebrew word but in order to clarify what the translators think the passage means. The result is that the NIV sometimes over-translates:

Ephesians 6:3

[ESV] "that it may go well with you and that you may live long in the land."

[NIV] "that it may go well with you and that you may enjoy long life on the earth."

The word translated in the ESV "live" is from the Greek word *eimi* meaning "to be" or "to live." It never means "to enjoy." The NIV has over-translated the text and changed its meaning from living a long life to enjoying one.

1 Corinthians 4:9

[ESV] "For I think that God has exhibited us apostles as last of all, like men sentenced to death, because we have become a spectacle to the world, to angels, and to men.

[NIV] "For it seems to me that God has put us apostles on display at the end of the procession, like men condemned to die in the arena. We have been made a spectacle to the whole universe, to angels as well as to men."

Most scholars agree that Paul's imagery of becoming a spectacle (*theatron*) is meant to invoke images of the gladiatorial arena. But the connection is not mentioned explicitly in the text. Being unsatisfied with an implied connection that readers might not notice, the NIV adds to the verse to explain the imagery with words like "procession" and "arena." This may have been the image in the back of Paul's mind, but it isn't what Paul said.

Allow me one more example of over-translation. In Colossians 3:1–2 Paul tells us (in the ESV) to "seek the things [*zēteite*] that are above" (v. 1) and to "set [our] minds on things that are above" (v. 2). I once heard a sermon on this text where the preacher was using the NIV, which has Paul saying, "set your *hearts* on things above" (v. 1) and "set your *minds* on things above" (v. 2). The preacher went on to talk about how we first set our hearts on things above, and then we set our minds on things above. But this is a point drawn from the NIV and not from the Greek. Paul, in verse 1, simply tells us *zēteite* ("seek"). The language of heart first and head second is found in the NIV, but not in the actual Bible text.

4. *The ESV engages in less under-translation.* In order to make the thought (not the words) of the biblical writers clearer, the NIV at times avoids theological words and important concepts found in the original languages.

One of the clearest examples is how the NIV translates *YHWH tsavaoth*. The ESV uses "LORD of hosts" to translate this common phrase, while the NIV uses "the LORD Almighty" and "God Almighty" because, according to the NIV Preface, "for most readers today the phrases 'the LORD of hosts' and 'God of hosts' have little meaning." It may be the case that "LORD of hosts" is not in many people's vocabularies, but shouldn't it be—at least for Christians? We lose something in translation when we no longer read "LORD of hosts." Yes, "LORD of hosts" implies that the Lord is Almighty, but *YHWH tsavaoth* also implies that our God is the Lord of heavenly hosts and military armies. The imagery of YHWH leading his people in battle or summoning legions of angels to deliver his people is lost when *tsavaoth* is not translated as "hosts" or "armies" (which is what the word means) but rather is translated as "Almighty" (which is not what the word denotes).

Another example where the NIV under-translates in an effort to be more understandable to modern readers is with the Greek word *hilasmos* (and its derivatives *hilasterion* and *hilaskomai*). Going back to the KJV, *hilasmos* has been usually translated as "propitiation." To propitiate means to placate, appease, or pacify. Christ is said to be our propitiation because he appeases the wrath of God (Rom. 3:25; Heb. 2:17; 1 John 2:2; 4:10). The ESV uses propitiation in all four verses. (The RSV, wary of notions of God's wrath, has "expiation," which refers simply to the removal of guilt. This is one of the reasons why evangelicals never embraced the RSV—another reason being Isaiah 7:14, where the RSV has "young woman" instead of "virgin.") The NIV, to be more easily understood, translates *hilasmos* (and its derivatives) as "sacrifice of atonement" (Rom. 3:25), "atonement" (Heb. 2:17), and "atoning sacrifice" (1 John 2:2; 4:10). So what's wrong with this? The problem with dropping "propitiation" is that (1) it makes it much more difficult for Christians to learn the meaning of and the concept behind this crucial word, (2) it is questionable whether "sacrifice of atonement," without explanation, will be readily understood by most Christians (or non-Christians) either, and (3) it deprives the church of important Christian vocabulary.

Let me give one more illustration of under-translating.

Acts 19:11

[ESV] "And God was doing extraordinary miracles by the hands [*tōn cheirōn*] of Paul . . . "

[NIV] "God did extraordinary miracles through Paul . . . "

For some reason, the NIV leaves out "the hands" even though it clearly is in the Greek. This happens in recounting other miracles as well (Mark 6:2; Acts 5:12; 14:3). I imagine the NIV felt that this was a circumlocution—a figure of speech where a number of words stand for something simple (i.e., "hands of Paul" = "Paul"). That's one possible interpretation. But it is more an interpretation than a translation. Why not leave "the hands" in the text? Perhaps God wants to make a point about the laying on of hands or the personal, physical nature of the miracles. Whatever the significance of "hands" may or may not be, the English reader should at least see that it is in the text and make his interpretations accordingly.

5. The ESV does a better job of translating important Greek or Hebrew words with the same English word throughout a passage or book. Every word in any language has a semantic range. This means every word can be translated with two or three or five or seven other words, and conversely that two or three words might all be translated by the same word, depending on the context. No translation project as big as the Bible can always translates "X-word" in Greek as "Q-word" in English. But an essentially literal translation will try, where possible and especially where it is important, to keep translation choices consistent according to the context.

For example, a key word in 1 John is the Greek word *menō*, which means "abide" or "remain." The verb occurs twenty-four times in 1 John. It is an important part of the overall argument of the epistle. The verb can easily be traced in the ESV with a good English concordance. Twenty-three out of twenty-four times, *menō* is translated as "abides" (or "abiding" or "abide"). By contrast, the NIV translates *menō* with five different words: "lives," "remains," "has," "continue," and "be."

A second example comes from the book of Ruth. In 2:12 (ESV), Boaz tells Ruth, "The LORD repay you for what you have done, and a full reward be given you by the LORD, the God of Israel, under whose wings [*kanaph*] you have come to take refuge." Then in 3:9, at the threshing floor, Ruth tells Boaz, "I am Ruth, your servant. Spread your wings [*kanaph*] over your servant, for you are a redeemer." Ruth is in effect telling Boaz to be the answer to his own prayer: "You told me to find refuge under the Lord's wings, so why don't you spread your wings over your servant and be my refuge, as you prayed?" The NIV has "under whose wings" in 2:12, but translates 3:9 as "the corner of your garment." This is an acceptable translation of *kanaph*, but translating the same Hebrew word with the same English word in 2:12 and 3:9, as the ESV does, helps the reader see the connection between Boaz's speech and Ruth's petition.

6. *The ESV retains more of the literary qualities of the Bible.* Leland Ryken, professor of English at Wheaton College and literary stylist for the ESV, argues that dynamic equivalent translations often don't do justice to the artistry, meter, subtlety, multi-layeredness, and concreteness found in the literature of the Bible, especially in poetry. By aiming first of all at what a modern reader can grasp, dynamic equivalent translations undermine the literary nature of the Bible. And "what is bad about an unliterary Bible?" asks Ryken. "It distorts the kind of book the Bible is (mainly an anthology of literary genres). It robs the Bible of the power that literature conveys. And it changes the nature of the writing that God by his Holy Spirit moved the biblical authors to produce."[4]

For example:

Psalm 35:10

[ESV] "All my bones [*etzem*] shall say, 'O Lᴏʀᴅ, who is like you . . . '"

[NIV] "My whole being will exclaim, 'Who is like you, O Lᴏʀᴅ?'"

The Hebrew word is "bones," not "being." It may be that "all my bones" is David's way of speaking of his "whole being," but when the text loses "bones" it trades a vivid poetic metaphor for an abstraction. Besides, does anyone really think that David's bones verbally spoke? Don't we intuitively understand that David uses "bones" to refer to

---

[4]Leland Ryken, *The Word of God in English: Criteria for Excellence in Bible Translation* (Wheaton, IL: Crossway, 2002), 171. Anyone who reads Ryken's book and this short booklet will notice that I owe much of my thinking on Bible translation and many of my examples to Ryken's excellent work.

the depth of feeling and intensity in his cry to God? The poetry of the NIV is not as good as the ESV, which better conveys a vivid, understandable Hebrew metaphor.

Psalm 78:33

[ESV] "So he made their days vanish like a breath [*hevel*], and their years in terror."

[NIV] "So he ended their days in futility and their years in terror."

The punch of the original is lost when "breath" is traded for "futility." The image of a puff of air vanishing as soon as it leaves the mouth is much more striking poetry than "futility."

Psalm 73:4, 7

[ESV] "For they have no pangs until death; their bodies are fat and sleek. . . . Their eyes swell out through fatness; their hearts overflow with follies.

[NIV] "They have no struggles; their bodies are healthy and strong. . . . From their callous hearts comes iniquity; the evil conceits of their minds know no limits."

Granted, the ESV translation is not as immediately understandable as the NIV, but this is not because the translation has failed. The difficulty is because this text is poetry and it's ancient. The imagery of a fat and sleek body may have to be explained to modern English readers—which is one of the reasons God has given the gift of teachers in the church—but it tells us something about ancient Hebrew culture that we don't get from words like "healthy" and "strong."[5] Plus, the NIV makes Asaph's poetry sound rather prosaic when "pangs until death" becomes "troubles" and hearts overflowing with follies become evil conceits of the mind that know no limits. And then there's the strange but important phrase, "Their eyes swell out through fatness." It's a grotesque picture of the prosperity of the wicked who are so swollen with luxury that it bulges out their eyes. This whole imagery is lost in the NIV.

Similarly, the essentially literal approach of the ESV in the book of Proverbs often sounds more, well, proverbial. The NIV often turns the aphoristic sound of proverbs into everyday conversation.

Proverbs 27:6

[ESV] "Faithful are the wounds of a friend; profuse are the kisses of an enemy."

[NIV] "Wounds from a friend can be trusted, but an enemy multiplies kisses."

Which sounds like a proverb and which sounds prosaic? The difference between the two translations is the dif-

---

[5]The NIV does include "their eyes bulge with fat" as an alternative marginal reading.

ference between "A stitch in time saves nine" and "If you stitch something now, you'll save yourself nine stitches later." Proverbs are supposed to sound different from everyday speech.

Even outside the Wisdom Literature, the ESV retains more of the concrete, vivid language of the original languages instead of trading it for interpretative abstraction.

1 Thessalonians 2:12

[ESV] "we exhorted each one of you and encouraged you and charged you to walk [*peripatein*] in a manner worthy of God . . . "

[NIV] "encouraging, comforting and urging you to live lives worthy of God . . . "

Isn't "walk in a manner worthy of God" more striking than "live lives worthy of God"? The verb conjures up images of physically walking away from evil and walking side by side with the Lord. Or to give one more example:

John 1:13

[ESV] "who were born, not of blood [*haimatōn*] nor of the will of the flesh [*thelēmatos sarkos*] nor of the will of man [*thelēmatos andros*], but of God."

[NIV] "children born not of natural descent, nor of human decision or a husband's will, but born of God."

Not only is the ESV a much more literal translation, it is still very understandable with the more concrete, earthier language of blood, will of the flesh, and will of man instead of the more abstract language of natural descent, human decision, and husband's will.

7. The ESV requires much less "correcting" in preaching. This may be the most important reason for switching to the ESV. I preached from the NIV for five years. It is a good translation in many respects, but it is difficult to preach from—especially if one wants to preach exegetically and with an eye to the original languages. There were a number of times over those five years when I had to un-explain the NIV in order to make a point in a sermon. Other times I had to simply skip a point I would have otherwise made because to get behind the NIV text in the sermon would have taken too much work.

To do careful preaching requires a more careful (i.e., more literal) text than the NIV. The other option is to frequently un-explain the English translation, which is a terrible habit. First, because it makes for laborious preaching. Second, because it leads people to think they need an "expert" in Greek or Hebrew to really explain the Bible. And third, because it causes people over time to come to their English Bibles with less confidence.

Let me give just three examples where the NIV has made my job as a preacher more difficult.

Luke 10:41–42

[ESV] "But the Lord answered her, 'Martha, Martha, you are anxious and troubled about many things, but one thing is necessary. Mary has chosen the good portion [*agathēn merida*], which will not be taken from her.'"

[NIV] "'Martha, Martha,' the Lord answered, 'You are worried and upset about many things, but only one thing is needed. Mary has chosen what is better, and it will not be taken away from her.'"

It may be true that sitting at the feet of Jesus is better than housework. That may even be a fair way to preach the text. But that isn't what Jesus says. He doesn't use the comparative "better," but the word "good" (*agathēn*). Jesus is defending Mary more than he is rebuking Martha for her preparations. In verse 40, Martha complains to Jesus that her sister isn't doing her share of the work. Jesus' reply is to inform Martha that Mary is not to be scolded, for she has chosen a good thing. Jesus doesn't say Mary chose what is better, only that she should not be faulted for ignoring the preparations, because sitting at his feet is a good thing that he won't take away from her by ordering her into the kitchen.

Ephesians 5:17–21

[ESV] "Therefore do not be foolish, but understand what the will of the Lord is. And do not get drunk with wine, for that is debauchery, but be filled with the Spirit, addressing one another in psalms and hymns and spiritual songs, singing and making melody to the Lord with all your heart, giving thanks always and for everything to God the Father in the name of our Lord Jesus Christ, submitting to one another out of reverence for Christ."

[NIV] "Therefore do not be foolish, but understand what the Lord's will is. Do not get drunk on wine, which leads to debauchery. Instead, be filled with the Spirit. Speak to one another with psalms, hymns and spiritual songs. Sing and make music in your heart to the Lord, always giving thanks to God the Father for everything, in the name of our Lord Jesus Christ. Submit to one another out of reverence for Christ."

This is a wonderful passage to preach from for many reasons, not least of which is the clear structure that Paul employs. Verse 18 begins with a negative command, "Do not get drunk with wine." Then he adds the positive command, "be filled with the Spirit." What Paul means by being filled with the Spirit is fleshed out by four participles in verses 19–21. A participle is a verbal adjective, often ending in "ing." The four participles—addressing, singing, giving thanks, submitting—are easily pointed out when preaching from the ESV. They are impossible to see in the NIV unless the text is un-explained. The NIV unnecessarily breaks 18–21 into four sentences instead of one, and translates three of the participles as commands ("Speak," "Sing," "Submit") and only one as a participle ("giving thanks").[6]

---

[6]The 2011 revision of the NIV changed "Speak" to "speaking."

It's true that participles can be translated as commands at times, but to do so here (inconsistently at that) ruins the obvious pattern. The pattern is further upset in the NIV by making verse 21 a new paragraph, as if submitting to one another introduces a new section but is not tied grammatically to the command "be filled with the Spirit." Without correcting the text, there's simply no way to preach on this passage from the NIV and use Paul's clear and compelling structure—a structure that greatly aids in understanding the passage.

Finally, although obviously it would not have been a part of our church's decision to switch to the ESV, let me give one example from the recently published 2011 edition of the NIV (see footnote 1, page 9). Compare the newer NIV renderings of 1 Timothy 1:12 with the older NIV and the ESV:

1 Timothy 2:12

[ESV] I do not permit a woman to teach or to exercise authority over a man; rather, she is to remain quiet.

[NIV 1984] I do not permit a woman to teach or to have authority over a man; she must be silent.

[TNIV (2005)] I do not permit a woman to teach or to assume authority over a man; she must be quiet.

[NIV 2011] I do not permit a woman to teach or to assume authority over a man; she must be quiet.

The 2005 and 2011 editions of the NIV have translated *authentein* as "to assume authority" instead of "to have authority." The TNIV added a footnote: "Or *teach a man in a domineering way;* or *teach or to exercise* (or *have*) *authority over a man.*" Unfortunately, NIV 2011 does not include this footnote.[7]

So, did Paul forbid women to "exercise" or "have" authority over a man (ESV; NIV 1984)? Or did he simply say they should not "assume" such authority? If the latter, then it suggests a woman is free to "exercise" authority over a man, as long as she doesn't wrongfully "assume" or usurp it. Obviously, this is relevant to the ongoing debate among evangelicals concerning the proper role of women in church leadership and in the marriage relationship. The ESV/NIV 1984 makes the focus of the prohibition authority itself, while the NIV 2011 translation leads one to think the problem is really with the illegitimate grabbing of power.

The latest scholarship comes down solidly on the side of the ESV and older NIV translation of *authentein* in 1 Timothy 2:12.[8] For whatever reason, the NIV 2011 translators, some of whom are complementarians, concluded otherwise. Any pastor who prefers the complementarian view of male and female roles but who preaches from the NIV is left with the task of "correcting" the translation of this key passage.

---

[7] Both the TNIV and the 2011 NIV include one other footnote which is not relevant to the present discussion.
[8] See Andreas J. Köstenberger and Thomas R. Schreiner, eds., *Women in the Church: An Analysis and Application of 1 Timothy 2:9–15*, 2nd ed. (Grand Rapids, Mich.: Baker, 2005), 39–51.

CONCLUSION

I want to reiterate that the NIV is not a bad translation. It was not wrong for my church to use the NIV, or for me to preach from it. Churches will continue to grow using the NIV. The lost will still be saved through the NIV and Christians will be built up in the faith with the NIV. I don't want to tear down the NIV.

I do, however, want to recommend the ESV. I believe it is a better translation based on better principles with a better sense of style and a better text from which to preach. I plan on using the ESV for many years in my personal study and writing and in my preaching and ministry at URC. If you already use the ESV, I hope this little booklet will bolster your confidence that the Bible you're reading is reliable, transparent, and essentially literal. If you currently use another translation, maybe even the NIV, I hope you will at least be open to a switch like my congregation was. You might even try out the ESV in your own personal and family devotions and group Bible study. And after that, consider giving the ESV a chance in your worship services.

Choosing a Bible translation is not a life or death decision, but it's far from a minor issue either. The Bible we study, the Bible used in our pulpits, the Bible read to our children is the Bible that will shape our vocabulary about God and even the way we think about God. The translation we choose can clarify difficult passages for us as the translators saw fit, or it can help us get closer to the world of the Bible, closer to the original languages, and closer to the figures and images of Scripture. The difference between the two approaches is not insignificant. "Man shall not live by bread alone, but by every word that comes from the mouth of God" (Matt. 4:4). So why not let these words—ancient, imaginative, and sometimes ambiguous—shine through as much as we can?